Ready to Stitch

Flowers

Lesley Taylor

SEARCHPRESS

First published in Great Britain 2014

Search Press Limited
Wellwood, North Farm Road,
Tunbridge Wells, Kent TN2 3DR

Text copyright © Lesley Taylor, 2014

Illustrations on pages 9–13 by Bess Harding

Photographs by Paul Bricknell at Search Press
Photographic Studios

Photographs and design copyright
© Search Press Ltd, 2014

All rights reserved. No part of this book, text, photographs or illustrations may be reproduced or transmitted in any form or by any means by print, photoprint, microfilm, microfiche, photocopier, internet or in any way known or as yet unknown, or stored in a retrieval system, without written permission obtained beforehand from Search Press.

ISBN: 978-1-84448-910-7

The Publishers and author can accept no responsibility for any consequences arising from the information, advice or instructions given in this publication.

Readers are permitted to reproduce any of the transfers or embroideries in this book for their personal use, or for the purpose of selling for charity, free of charge and without the prior permission of the Publishers. Any use of the transfers or embroideries for commercial purposes is not permitted without the prior permission of the Publishers.

Suppliers
All of the threads used in the book were kindly supplied by DMC Creative World. Visit www.dmc.com for details of your nearest stockist. If you have any difficulty obtaining any of the other materials and equipment mentioned in this book, please visit the Search Press website: www.searchpress.com.

Publishers' notes
All the embroideries in this book were made by the author, Lesley Taylor, using threads supplied by DMC.

Please note: to remove the transfers you want to use from the book, cut round them carefully. They can be stored in the pocket at the back of the book and used several times.

Printed in China

The images used in this book were previously published in:

The Design Library: Flower Designs by Judy Balchin, transfer sheets 3, 5 (top & left), 6, 7, 14 (top), 17, 18 (right) and 21 (right)

The Design Library: Heart & Flower Designs by Judy Balchin, transfer sheets 1, 4 (right) and 11 (bottom)

Design Source Book: Art Nouveau Borders & Motifs by Judy Balchin, transfer sheets 21 (bottom left), 23 (middle left) and 27

Design Source Book: Floral Borders & Motifs by Penny Brown, transfer sheets 4 (left), 5 (bottom right), 9 (left), 10, 11 (top), 12 (bottom left), 22, 23 (top right, bottom right, bottom left), 24, 25, 26 and 31

Design Source Book: Garden Flower Designs by Polly Pinder, transfer sheets 2, 8, 12 (top & bottom right), 13, 14 (bottom), 15, 16, 18 (left), 19 (middle & top), 20, 21 (top left), 28 (bottom), 29, 30 and 32

Design Source Book: Traditional Japanese Designs by Polly Pinder, transfer sheets 19 (top) and 28 (top)

Design Source Book: Tudor Designs by Polly Pinder, transfer sheet 9 (right)

Dedication
For Gary, Emily and Mum

Acknowledgements
I would like to thank all my family and friends, especially my sister Sara, for their support while writing this book. In particular, I would like to thank Liz at Quilty Pleasures, Brighton for her amazing range of lovely patchwork fabrics; Cara at DMC for providing all the threads for the samples and projects; and Katie, Roz, Marrianne and Juan at Search Press for all their support and guidance. Also thank you to Pam Watts for her recommendation, without whom this journey wouldn't have begun.

A special thank you to Mum who, although she didn't see this book, started me on my creative path in life. Thank you to Emily for helping me to find the words and your continued support. Finally a very big thank you must go to Gary for all the help and encouragement that he has given me.

Contents

Introduction

Embroidery is the art of decorating the surface of fabric with needle and thread and, along with many other crafts, is currently enjoying a revival. Fun, relaxing and portable, it's the perfect way to explore your creativity without the need for expensive equipment or a generous space in which to work, and its modern appeal suits all tastes and abilities.

How to use this book

In this book, I've taken just 10 simple stitches and used them in a variety of colours and combinations to embroider 74 different flower designs, each of which is shown on one of the samplers on pages 16–81. All the designs are also provided as transfers on the detachable sheets at the back of the book.

If you are new to embroidery, you may find it useful to start by reading through the sections at the start of the book and practising the stitches before embarking on an embroidery; otherwise simply choose your design from the samplers, find the corresponding transfer sheet and iron the design on to your fabric following the instructions on page 14.

Each sampler is accompanied by notes on the threads, colours and stitches used so that you can, if you wish, reproduce the designs exactly. Alternatively, simply use them as a source of ideas, inspiration and guidance for creating embroidered designs of your own – you'll be amazed at the different looks you can achieve just by changing the thread colours and stitches used.

On pages 82–95 are some ideas for how to use the embroideries to brighten, transform or personalise an otherwise plain and simple fabric item, for example a child's denim dress, a tea cosy or a sun hat. Whatever you choose to embroider, don't be afraid to try out different colours and stitch combinations to create something unique, and, above all, have fun while you are doing it!

What you need

Very little is needed to start embroidery – just some fabric, thread, a needle, pins, an embroidery hoop and a pair of scissors.

Needles

The best needles to use are embroidery or crewel needles. These are fine, sharp needles with a large eye, sized from 1 to 10; the higher the number the finer the needle. As a general guide use the higher numbers on finer fabrics and the lower numbers on heavier fabrics. Chenille needles are also useful for working with thicker threads and heavier fabrics. They come in sizes 14 to 26. A blunt-ended tapestry needle is also a useful tool for darning through any stray ends.

It is worth buying good-quality needles as the cheaper ones can rub the thread as it passes through the eye, causing it to shred.

Scissors

A small pair of sharp scissors for cutting threads is essential. A pair of dressmakers' shears will be useful for cutting fabric or you may prefer to use a rotary cutter and mat. Use an old pair of scissors to cut around the transfers.

Pins

Dressmaking pins are useful to secure the transfer to the fabric when ironing off the design.

Fabric

Many different types of fabric can be used for hand embroidery. However, it is best to use plain-weave fabrics, which include cotton, linen, wool, dressmaking and patchwork fabric and some lightweight furnishing fabrics.

Synthetic and stretch fabrics can be difficult to work with and very often need to be backed with a stabiliser such as Stitch and Tear. This is a soft, paper-like fabric that can be torn away after you have stitched your design. It is available from most craft shops and on-line suppliers.

Smooth fabrics are easier to stitch on to than textured ones. It is difficult to transfer the designs on to an uneven surface and the stitching can look untidy and disappear into the weave.

Embroidery threads

All of the samplers and projects in this book have been worked with DMC stranded cottons, though other brands can be used, and feel free to experiment with other thread types. Some suitable ones are listed below.

Stranded cottons are available in skeins and come in a huge range of colours, including a variegated variety known as 'colour variation thread'. Stranded cotton is made up of six strands that can be separated, making it suitable for use with most fabrics. Try combining threads from different-coloured stranded cottons to make your work more individual.

Metallic threads also come in a skein and can be separated and used with other stranded threads to add a sparkly finish.

Cotton perle is a twisted thread with a beautiful lustre, and comes in four weights: 3, 5, 8 and 12. It cannot be divided into strands. Like stranded cotton, it is also available in a variegated variety.

Crewel wool is a lightweight wool specially designed for embroidery. It can be divided into strands for hand embroidery or mixed with other stranded threads. It is a heavier thread than the ones mentioned above and is perfect for use on heavier-weight fabrics.

Embroidery hoops

An embroidery hoop keeps your fabric taut while you are stitching and helps prevent the stitches from puckering the fabric, which gives an untidy finish to your work. Hoops come in a range of sizes and are usually wooden with a tension screw on the outer ring. This screw allows you to adjust the tension on the outer ring once the fabric is secured in the hoop. Plastic flexi hoops and spring hoops are also available.

Always try to use a hoop that will hold the complete design comfortably. If you need to keep repositioning the hoop, it may leave marks on the fabric.

Stitches used

I've used just 10 simple embroidery stitches to produce all of the designs in this book. Don't be afraid to experiment and try different combinations of stitches, thread colours and fabrics – you will be amazed by their versatility and the wonderful effects you can achieve.

Starting to stitch

Bring your needle and thread up through the fabric on the spot where you are going to place your first stitch. You will need to hold the end of the thread to stop it going right through (1). Make sure your first three or four stitches go over the starting thread on the wrong side of the fabric to secure it (2).

Alternatively, make a small knot at the end of your thread and insert the needle down into the fabric about 2.5cm (1in) away from where your first stitch will be placed. It must be along the line of your first few stitches. Bring the needle up where you are going to start stitching (3). Embroider the first few stitches up to the knot, making sure you have stitched over the starting thread on the back of your work. You can now snip off the knot and continue stitching (4).

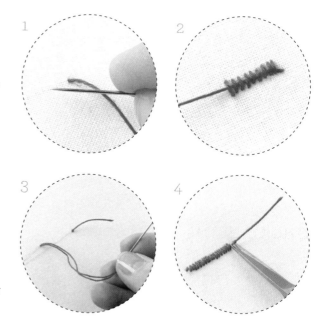

Fastening off a thread

To fasten off a thread, slip the needle through the back of the stitches you have just worked (5), pull the thread through and snip off the tail (6). To rejoin a thread, slip the thread through the back of the same stitches and continue stitching.

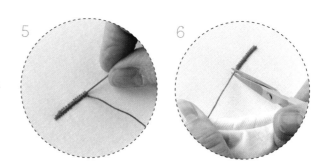

Running stitch

This is perhaps the simplest of embroidery stitches. Although not used in the designs, it has been used as a decorative stitch in some of the projects. It can be used as an outline stitch or as a foundation for other stitches.

Bring the needle up at A and insert it at B and bring it up again at C. Continue along the stitch line, leaving an equal space between the stitches.

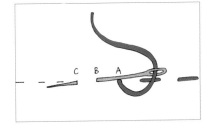

Long stitch

This simple stitch can been used on its own to create veins on leaves and petals. It is a single, long running stitch.

Bring the needle up at A and insert it at B to create a single, long stitch. Make further stitches as required.

Back stitch

Back stitch can be used for both curved and straight lines. It is the easiest stitch to use for outlining a shape and is less heavy than chain stitch or stem stitch.

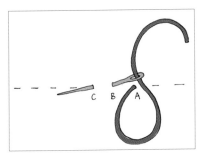

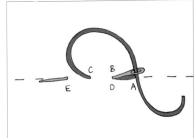

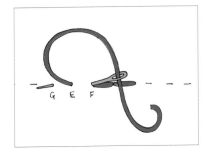

1 Bring the needle up at A and pull the thread through. Insert the needle at B and bring it through at C. Pull the thread through the fabric.

2 Insert the needle at D and bring it up at E. Pull the thread through.

3 Insert the needle at F and bring it up at G. Continue working along the stitch line until it is completed. To finish off, thread your needle through the stitches on the wrong side of your work.

Chain stitch

Chain stitch can be used as an outline stitch or worked side to side as a filling stitch.

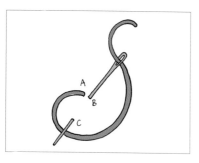

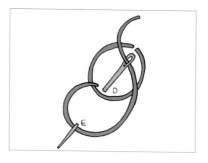

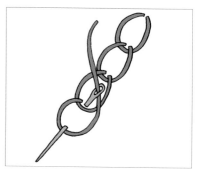

1 Bring the needle up through the fabric at A and pull the thread through. Insert the needle at B, as close as possible to A, and bring it up at C. Keep the thread under the needle. Pull the thread through gently to form the first chain.

2 Insert the needle at D, as close as possible to C, and bring the needle up at E. Keeping the thread under the needle, pull the thread through gently to form the second chain.

3 Continue in this way, making evenly sized chain stitches, until the line of stitching is complete.

French knots

French knots can be worked singly or in clusters. They are very useful for creating a pretty textured effect within a shape. They are particularly good for creating flower centres.

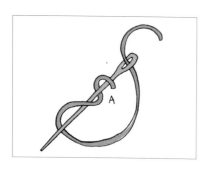

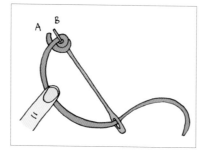

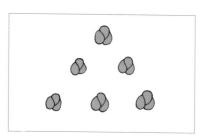

1 Bring the thread through where the knot is required, at A. Holding the thread between your thumb and finger, wrap it around the needle twice.

2 Hold the thread firmly with your thumb and turn the needle back to A. Insert it as close to A as possible, at B, and pull the thread through to form a knot.

3 Make as many knots as you need. Make a small stitch on the wrong side of the fabric before fastening off.

Lazy daisy (detached chain) stitch

This very popular stitch is used to make a simple daisy design. It can also be used to fill a space when a bolder effect is required.

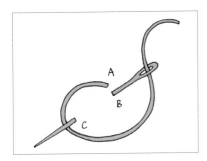 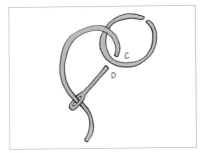 

1 Bring the thread through at A and, securing the thread with your thumb, insert the needle at B, as close to A as possible. Bring the needle through at C. Pull the thread through gently to create a loop.

2 Insert the needle at D, making sure you pass the thread over the loop, to secure.

3 Make as many stitches as required, then make a small stitch on the wrong side of your work to secure.

Blanket stitch

Blanket stitches can be worked widely spaced to form a border or closely together to form a filling stitch. It can be worked into rounds or curved areas too.

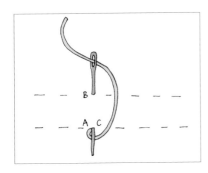 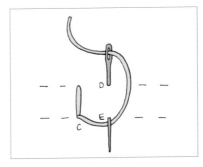 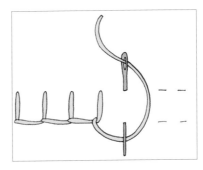

1 Bring the needle up through the fabric at A and pull the thread through. Take it back down at B and up at C, as close as possible to A. Take care to keep the thread under the needle. Use your thumb to secure the thread. Pull the thread through gently to form the first stitch.

2 Leaving the required space between stitches, insert the needle at D and come up at E, keeping the thread under the needle while pulling the thread through.

3 Repeat steps 1 and 2. Try not to pull the stitches too tightly as this can cause the stitch to distort and the fabric to pucker. To finish, make a small stitch to the right of the final loop, take the thread to the wrong side of the fabric and fasten off.

Seeding stitch

This stitch is particularly easy to work. It can be stitched fairly openly or worked much closer together to create tight clusters. The stitches themselves can be placed at different angles to create a random effect or can be worked in one direction only.

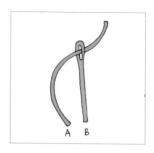

1 Bring the needle up at A and insert it at B to create a tiny stitch.

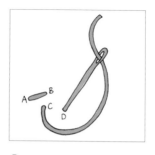

2 Bring the needle up at C and insert it at D to make a second stitch at a different angle.

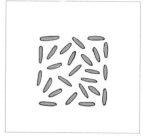

3 Continue placing the stitches randomly until the area is filled.

Long and short stitch

This stitch is sometimes used where the area to be filled is too large for satin stitch, or where you want to achieve a shaded effect. You can adjust the length of the stitches to fit the shape you are filling. I sometimes find it easier to mark out the area that is to be filled when laying down the foundation row for this stitch. You can use a water-soluble pencil or an ordinary one: as the shape is going to be filled with stitching, it won't show.

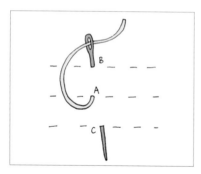

1 Bring the needle through at A and pull the thread through. Insert it at B to form a short stitch. Come up again at C.

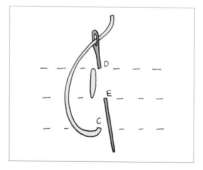

2 Insert the needle at D, as close to B as possible, to form the long stitch. Come up again at E. Continue to the end of the row.

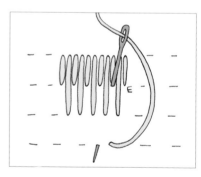

3 For the second row, work long stitches underneath each of the short stitches in row 1, as shown above.

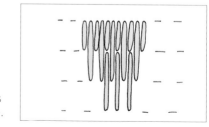

4 Continue with as many rows as you need until the design is complete.

Satin stitch

Satin stitch is perhaps the most popular stitch for filling in the solid areas on a design. By adjusting the length of the stitches it can be worked to fit most shapes. Take care when placing your needle so that you get an even edge.

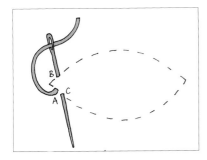 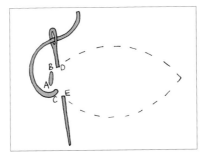 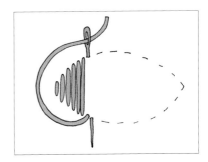

1 Bring your thread up at A, on the edge of the shape, and insert the needle at B. Pull the thread through gently. Pulling the thread too tightly will cause the fabric to pucker. Bring the needle up at C working as close to A as possible.

2 Take the needle down at D, as close as possible to B, and bring it back through at E, next to C. Pull the thread through gently to make a stitch that lies next to the first stitch, without overlapping it.

3 Continue as above until the shape is filled. Pass the needle through to the back of the work to fasten off.

Stem stitch

Stem stitch can be worked as an outline stitch or a filling stitch, when rows are laid down close together. As the name suggests, it is particularly effective when worked along the stems of flowers and plants.

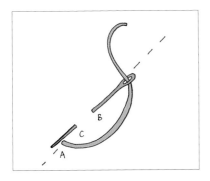 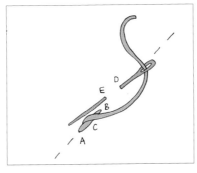 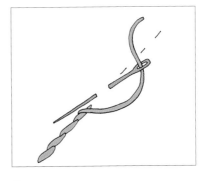

1 Bring the thread through at A and hold it down with your thumb to form a loop. Insert the needle at B and bring it out at C, between A and B.

2 Pull the thread through to make the first stitch. Hold the working thread down with your thumb as before. Insert the needle at D and bring it out at E, slightly to the side of B.

3 Continue until the line of stitching is complete. If using as a filling stitch, simply work another row next to the first and repeat until the area is filled.

Transferring the designs

The transfer sheets for all the designs are at the back of this book. You can cut around the smaller flowers if you are using them individually, but make sure you leave as much paper as possible around the edge. When you have used the transfer, store it in the pocket on the back cover to keep it safe until you wish to use it again. Transfer the designs using an ordinary iron (without steam) set on 'cotton'. Make sure you use a fabric that is not damaged by this heat. If possible, use a spare piece of your fabric to check before you start.

1 Pin the transfer ink-side down on the right side of the fabric where you want the design to be.

2 Place the iron over the transfer area and leave for about 10 seconds. Do not move the iron as this may blur the image. Carefully lift a corner of the transfer to make sure it has printed on to the fabric. If not, leave the iron for a little longer or increase the temperature and try again.

3 When you are happy that the design has transferred successfully, remove the transfer. Your design is now ready to be placed in the embroidery hoop for stitching.

Using dark and heavily patterned fabrics

If your fabric is dark or has a heavy all-over pattern, this will make it hard to see the transferred outline. To overcome this problem you can embroider the design on to a piece of plain or lighter-coloured fabric and then sew it on to the darker fabric. Alternatively, the transfer can be ironed on to a woven water-soluble fabric; not the plastic types as these will melt with the heat of the iron. This can then be tacked on to the item to be stitched and washed away when the stitching has been completed.

Using an embroidery hoop

Make sure the embroidery hoop is large enough to include the whole of the design within the frame, but not so large that there is insufficient fabric around the outside to secure it. Binding the inner hoop will not only help to hold the fabric more firmly but also avoid the frame marking the fabric. Use a woven tape 2.5cm (1in) wide.

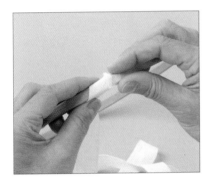

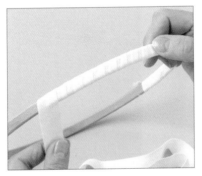

1 Tape the end of the binding at a 45° angle. Secure the end by using a little piece of masking tape.

2 Wrap the tape around the hoop with one hand whilst using your thumb on the other hand to keep the tape secure. You need to pull the tape fairly tight to stop it sagging or any gaps appearing.

3 When you reach the end remove the masking tape and wrap the remaining tape over the gap and a couple more times to make sure the ends overlap. Stitch the ends together and trim off any surplus.

4 Lay the bound inner hoop on a firm surface. Place the fabric over the hoop with the design facing upwards. Keeping the tension screw at the top, put the outer ring over the top and press down to sandwich the fabric between the inner and outer hoops.

5 Tighten the tension screw (a small screwdriver is sometimes useful here).

6 Holding the hoop in one hand, gently ease out any slack in the fabric. The fabric should now be nice and tight in the frame.

The samplers

These samplers have been stitched using different combinations of stitches, threads and thread colours to show the huge range of effects that can be achieved. Some of the designs have been filled in completely with stitch, some have been simply outlined, and others use a combination of the two.

Each of the samplers has a corresponding transfer sheet, and is accompanied by notes on the stitches, thread colours and the number of strands used, including the DMC colour codes. These notes will allow you to reproduce the designs exactly as shown, using either DMC threads or any suitable alternatives. You can also use the samplers as inspiration for creating your own embroideries by simply changing the stitches and colours used.

All of the samplers have been worked on plain white cotton fabric using DMC stranded cotton threads, both plain and variegated. Where a variegated thread has been used, you will obtain a slightly different shading effect from the one shown in the picture and, similarly, if you use threads other than DMC, the colours may vary slightly.

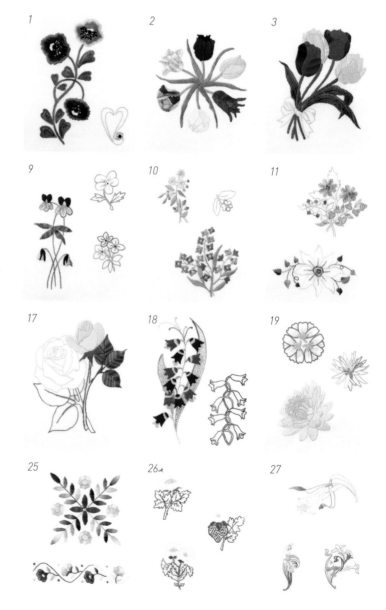

Getting started

Once you have selected your design, transfer it to your fabric (see page 14) and secure it in an embroidery hoop (see page 15). You are then ready to start. Begin by gathering together the tools and threads you need (see pages 6–7), then select which stitch you want to start with. Start in the centre of the design and work outwards, as this will give a neater finish. Follow the printed lines closely and make sure they are covered as much as possible by the stitching. Although they will fade with washing, they may not disappear completely.

Try to keep the length of thread you use to approximately 45cm (18in). If the thread twists while you are stitching, try holding your work upside down in the hoop so that the weight of the needle unravels the twist.

Note that the thread numbers provided refer to DMC threads used; 'var' after the number means it is a variegated (or 'colour variation') thread.

Thread key

DMC colours used:

███	310
███	3799
███	211
███	208
███	550
███	4045 (var)

Stitches and threads used:

██ ██ Flower centres worked with satin stitch using 3 strands of 310; satin stitch using 3 strands of 3799; and French knots using 3 strands of 310.

██ ██ ██ Petals worked with long and short stitch using 211, 208 and 550 (3 strands of each colour).

██ Leaves worked with chain stitch using 3 strands of 4045.

██ Stems worked with stem stitch using 2 strands of 4045.

Stitches and threads used:

██ Heart outlined with chain stitch using 3 strands of 211.

██ Flower centre worked with French knots using 2 strands of 310.

██ Petals outlined with back stitch using 2 strands of 208.

Thread key

DMC colours used:

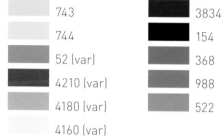

743
744
52 (var)
4210 (var)
4180 (var)
4160 (var)

3834
154
368
988
522

Stitches and threads used for stems and leaves:

 Stems worked with satin stitch using 2 strands of 522.

Leaf tips worked with satin stitch using 2 strands of 368.

Main leaves worked with satin stitch using 1 strand of 522 and 1 strand of 988, worked together in the needle.

Stitches and threads used for flowers:

Petals worked with satin stitch and back stitch using 2 strands of 154 and 2 strands of 3834.

Petals worked with back stitch using 2 strands of 744; and satin stitch using 2 strands of 743, and 1 strand of 743 and 1 of 744 worked together in the needle.

Petals worked with satin stitch using 2 strands of 4210.

Petals worked with satin stitch using 2 strands of 4160.

Petals worked with satin stitch using 2 strands of 52.

Petals worked with satin stitch using 2 strands of 4180.

3

Thread key

DMC colours used:

■	115 (var)
■	321
■	743
■	4075 (var)
■	367
■	936
■	4150 (var)

Stitches and threads used:

■ ■ ■ ■ Flowers worked with satin stitch using 743 and 4075 for yellow flowers and 115 and 321 for red flowers (3 strands of each colour).

■ Stems worked with stem stitch using 3 strands of 367.

■ ■ Leaves worked with long and short stitch using 367 and 936 in alternate rows (2 strands of each colour).

■ Bow worked with chain stitch using 2 strands of 4150.

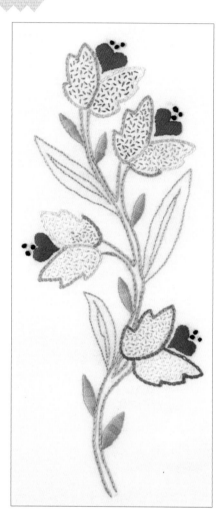

4

Thread key

DMC colours used:

■	154
■	917
■	4050 (var)
■	48 (var)

Stitches and threads used:

■ Stamens worked with three French knots per flower using 2 strands of 154.

■ Hearts worked with satin stitch using 2 strands of 917.

■ Petals outlined with chain stitch using 2 strands of 48.

■ Petals filled with seed stitch using 2 strands of 48.

■ Large leaves outlined with back stitch using 2 strands of 4050.

■ Small leaves worked with satin stitch using 2 strands of 4050.

■ Stems worked with chain stitch using 2 strands of 4050.

Stitches and threads used:

■ Flower centre worked with satin stitch using 1 strand of 154.

■ ■ Petals outlined with chain stitch using 917 and 48 (1 strand of each colour).

■ Leaves outlined with back stitch using 1 strand of 4050.

■ Stem outlined with chain stitch using 1 strand of 4050.

Stitches and threads used:

◼◼ Flowers worked with satin stitch using 554 and 553 (2 strands of each colour).

◼ Leaves and sepals worked with satin stitch using 2 strands of 368.

◼ Stems worked with stem stitch using 2 strands of 368.

◼ Tendrils worked with back stitch using 1 strand of 368.

Thread key

DMC colours used:

◼ 554
◼ 553
◼ 341
◼ 340
◼ 368

Stitches and threads used:

◼◼ Flowers worked with satin stitch using 341 and 340 (2 strands of each colour).

◼ Leaves and sepals worked with satin stitch using 2 strands of 368.

◼ Stems worked with stem stitch using 2 strands of 368.

◼ Tendrils worked with back stitch using 1 strand of 368.

Stitches and threads used:

◼◼ Flowers worked with satin stitch using 554 and 553 (2 strands of each colour).

◼ Leaves and sepals worked with satin stitch using 2 strands of 368.

◼ Stems worked with stem stitch using 2 strands of 368.

6

Thread key

DMC colours used:

■	902
■	3726
■	3727
■	3051
■	3012
■	3855

Stitches and threads used:

■■■ Outer edge of main petal worked in long and short stitch using (from the outer edge in towards the centre of the petal) 902, 3726 and 3727 (3 strands of each colour).

■ Central vein on main petal worked with stem stitch using 3 strands of 3855.

■ Two small red petals worked in satin stitch using 3 strands of 902.

■ Two large lower petals outlined with chain stitch using 3 strands of 902.

■■ Inner pattern on petals worked in lazy daisy stitch using 3855 and 3727 (3 strands of each colour).

■■ Leaves worked with satin stitch, one using 3012 and two using 3051 (3 strands of each colour).

7

Thread key

DMC colours used:

742

4240 (var)

158

3052

Stitches and threads used:

Filled areas of petals worked with satin stitch using 3 strands of 4240.

Petal outline worked with stem stitch using 3 strands of 158.

Pattern in centre of flower worked in stem stitch and seed stitch using 3 strands of 4240.

Yellow part ('beard') in centre of flower worked in satin stitch and back stitch using 3 strands of 742.

Stem worked in stem stitch using 3 strands of 3052.

8

Thread key

DMC colours used:

- 742
- 744
- 4075 (var)
- 743
- 522

Stitches and threads used:

Stigma and stamens in centre of flower worked with French knots using 2 strands of 742.

Folded edge of trumpet worked with satin stitch using 2 strands of 744.

Base of trumpet worked with satin stitch using 2 strands of 4075.

Rim of trumpet outlined with back stitch using 2 strands of 4075.

Petals outlined with stem stitch using 2 strands of 4075.

Folded edges of petals worked with satin stitch using 2 strands of 744.

Lines on petals worked with stem stitch using 2 strands of 4075.

Stitches and threads used:

Flower centres worked with lazy daisy stitch using 2 strands of 743.

Trumpets outlined with chain stitch using 2 strands of 742.

Petals worked with satin stitch using 2 strands of 4075.

Leaf outlines and veins worked with back stitch using 2 strands of 522.

9

Stitches and threads used:

■ Top two petals of open flowers worked with satin stitch using 2 strands of 550.

■■ Lower three petals of open flowers outlined with chain stitch using 2 strands of 52; lines on these petals worked with straight stitch using 1 strand of 550.

■ Centres of open flowers worked with satin stitch and lazy daisy stitch using 2 strands of 4128.

■■ Closed flowers worked with satin stitch using 550 and 52 (2 strands of each colour).

■ Leaves worked with satin stitch using 2 strands of 4045.

■ Stems worked with stem stitch using 2 strands of 4045.

Thread key

DMC colours used:

■ 550
■ 4128 (var)
■ 4045 (var)
■ 52 (var)
■ 310
■ 3836
■ 327

Stitches and threads used (left):

■■■ Flowers outlined with back stitch using 3836, 550 and 327 (2 strands of each colour).

■■ Flower centres worked with a single French knot using 2 strands of 310; and back stitch using 1 strand of 4128.

■ Stems and leaves outlined with back stitch using 1 strand of 4045.

Stitches and threads used (above):

■ Petals outlined with chain stitch; and lines on these petals worked with back stitch using 2 strands of 4128.

■ Flower centre worked with a single French knot using 2 strands of 310.

■ Stems and leaves outlined with back stitch using 2 strands of 4045.

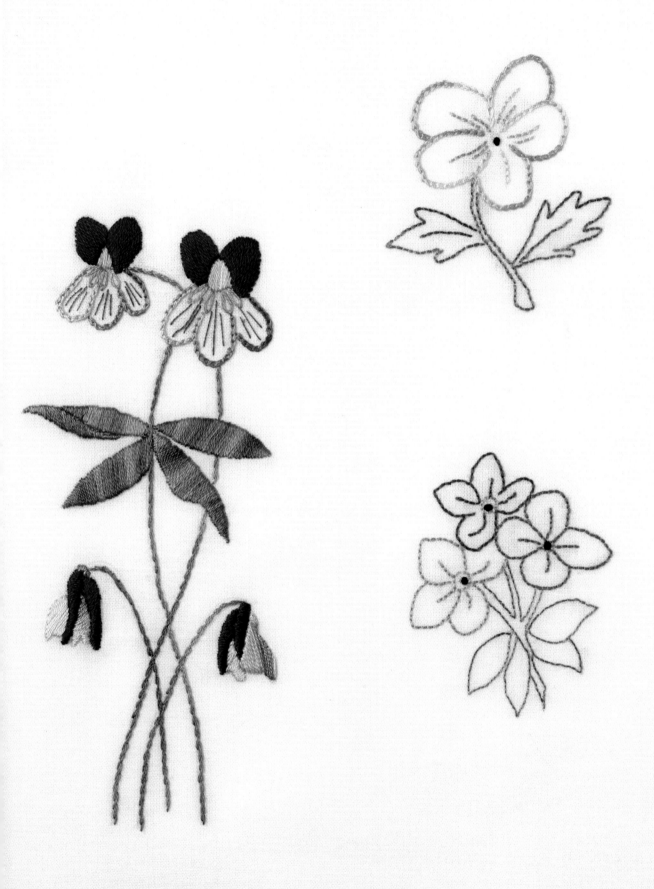

10

Stitches and threads used:

Flowers worked with satin stitch using 4215 and 322 (2 strands of each colour).

Flower centres worked with single French knots using 2 strands of 742.

Leaves worked with satin stitch using 2 strands of 368.

Main stems worked with stem stitch and fine stems with back stitch using 2 strands of 368.

Thread key

DMC colours used:

742

4215 (var)

322

554

368

Stitches and threads used:

Top three flowers worked with lazy daisy stitch using 554 and 4215 (2 strands of each colour); outlines worked with back stitch using 2 strands of 554.

Flower centres worked with single French knots using 2 strands of 742.

Round buds worked with satin stitch using 2 strands of 4215.

Lower buds worked with satin stitch using 2 strands of 322.

Leaves and sepals worked with satin stitch using 2 strands of 368.

Stems worked with back stitch using 2 strands of 368.

Stitches and threads used:

Flower outlined with chain stitch using 2 strands of 4215.

Flower centre worked with French knots using 3 strands of 742.

Leaves and stem outlined with back stitch using 2 strands of 368.

11

Thread key

DMC colours used:

▉	4140 (var)
▉	4070 (var)
▉	4130 (var)
▉	4128 (var)
▉	4090 (var)
▉	92 (var)

Stitches and threads used:

▉ Petals of two large flowers worked with lazy daisy stitch using 3 strands of 4128.

▉ Flower centres worked with French knots using 2 strands of 4140.

▉ Nuts worked with satin stitch using 2 strands of 4130.

▉ Berries outlined with back stitch and filled with seed stitch using 2 strands of 4130.

▉ Leaves and stems worked with satin stitch and back stitch using 2 strands of 4070.

Stitches and threads used:

▉ Petals outlined with stem stitch using 2 strands of 4090.

▉▉ Flower centre worked with cluster of French knots using 2 strands of 4140, surrounded by ring of French knots using 2 strands of 4130; space in between filled with seed stitch using 2 strands of 4140.

▉ Veins on petals worked with back stitch using 2 strands of 4128.

▉ Leaves and stems worked with satin stitch and back stitch using 2 strands of 92.

12

Thread key

DMC colours used:

- 917
- 605
- 603
- 3348

Stitches and threads used:

Flower centres worked with French knots and long stitch using 2 strands of 917.

Petals outlined with chain stitch using 2 strands of 603.

Stitches and threads used:

Flower centres worked with French knots and long stitch using 2 strands of 917.

Petals outlined with stem stitch using 603 and 605 (2 strands of each colour).

Folded edges of petals worked with satin stitch using 2 strands of 605.

Buds worked with satin stitch using 2 strands of 603.

Sepals at base of buds worked with satin stitch using 2 strands of 3348.

Stem and closed buds outlined with back stitch using 2 strands of 3348.

Stitches and threads used:

Flower centres worked with satin stitch using 2 strands of 917.

Petals worked with satin stitch using 2 strands of 605.

Buds worked with satin stitch using 2 strands of 917.

Leaves, sepals and stems worked with satin stitch and back stitch using 2 strands of 3348.

13

Stitches and threads used:

■ ■ Centres of middle and left-hand flowers worked with French knots; inner cluster using 3857 and outer ring using 4140 (2 strands of each colour).

■ Centre of right-hand flower worked with satin stitch using 2 strands of 4124.

■ Petals worked with chain stitch (left-hand flower) and satin stitch (middle and right-hand flowers) using 2 strands of 4124.

■ Stems and leaves outlined with back stitch using 2 strands of 988.

Thread key

DMC colours used:

■ 4140 (var)
■ 3857
■ 4124 (var)
■ 4130 (var)
■ 988

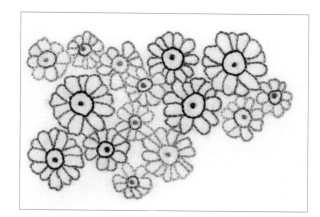

Stitches and threads used:

 ■ Centres of orange flowers worked with a single French knot and a ring of back stitch using 3 strands of 4140.

■ Petals of orange flowers worked with back stitch using 3 strands of 4124.

 ■ Centres of red/brown flowers worked with a single French knot and a ring of back stitch using 3 strands of 3857.

■ Petals of red/brown flowers worked with back stitch using 3 strands of 4130.

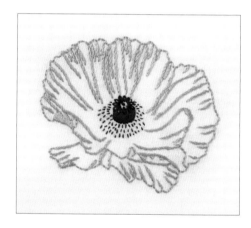

14

Thread key

DMC colours used:

■	310
■	321
■	115 (var)
■	936
■	902
■	352

Stitches and threads used:

■ Flower centre worked with lazy daisy stitch and back stitch using 3 strands of 310.

■ Small folds radiating from centre of flower worked with stem stitch using 3 strands of 115.

■ Petals outlined with back stitch using 3 strands of 321.

■ Folded edges of petals worked with satin stitch using 3 strands of 115.

■ Stem worked with satin stitch using 3 strands of 936.

Stitches and threads used:

■ Flower centre (capsule) worked with lazy daisy stitch, satin stitch and a single French knot using 2 strands of 902.

■ Stamens worked with seed stitch using 2 strands of 902.

■ Top edges of petals worked with back stitch using 3 strands of 352.

■ Edges and folds of petals worked with stem stitch using 3 strands of 352.

■ Folded edges of petals filled with satin stitch using 3 strands of 352.

15

Thread key

DMC colours used:

 666

3053

Stitches and threads used:

Flower petals outlined with back stitch using 2 strands of 666.

Folds in petals worked with long stitch using 2 strands of 666.

Buds worked with satin stitch using 2 strands of 666.

Sepals around buds worked with satin stitch using 3 strands of 3053.

Stems worked with stem stitch using 3 strands of 3053.

Hairs on stems worked with single, small stitches using 1 strand of 3053.

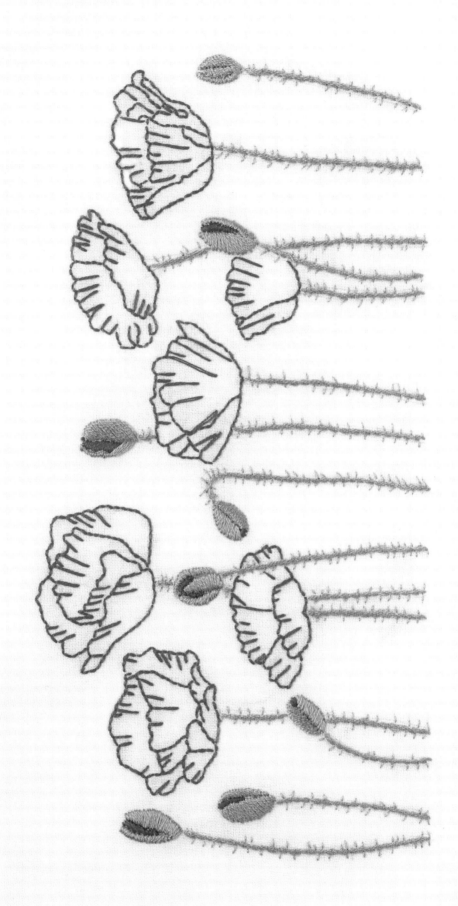

16

Thread key

DMC colours used:

 115 (var)

4045 (var)

Stitches and threads used:

Rose petals outlined with chain stitch using 2 strands of 115.

Large leaves outlined with chain stitch using 2 strands of 4045.

Stems and small leaves outlined with back stitch using 2 strands of 4045.

17

Thread key

DMC colours used:

▢	3855
▨	4045 (var)
■	367

Stitches and threads used:

▢ Smaller flower (right) worked with satin stitch; larger flower (left) outlined with back stitch using 3 strands of 3855.

▨ Leaves of smaller flower worked with satin stitch using 3 strands of 4045.

■ Stem of smaller flower outlined with stem stitch using 3 strands of 367.

■ Sepals of smaller flower worked with satin stitch using 3 strands of 367.

■ Stem and leaves of larger flower outlined with back stitch using 2 strands of 4045.

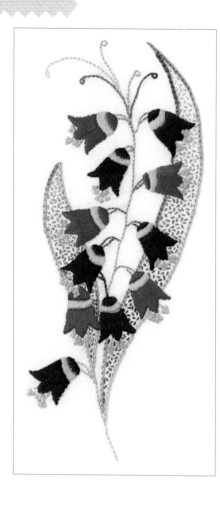

18

Thread key

DMC colours used:

▨	742
▨	917
▨	550
▨	92 (var)

Stitches and threads used:

▨ Stamens worked with French knots using 3 strands of 742.

▨▨▨ Flowers worked with satin stitch using 917, 550 and 742 (3 strands of each colour).

▨ Stems worked with back stitch using 3 strands of 92.

▨ Leaves outlined with chain stitch and filled with seed stitch using 3 strands of 92.

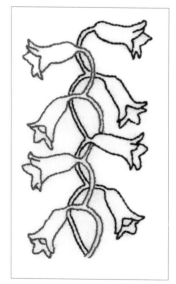

Stitches and threads used:

▨ Left-hand flower outlined with back stitch using 3 strands of 917.

▨ Right-hand flower outlined with back stitch using 3 strands of 550.

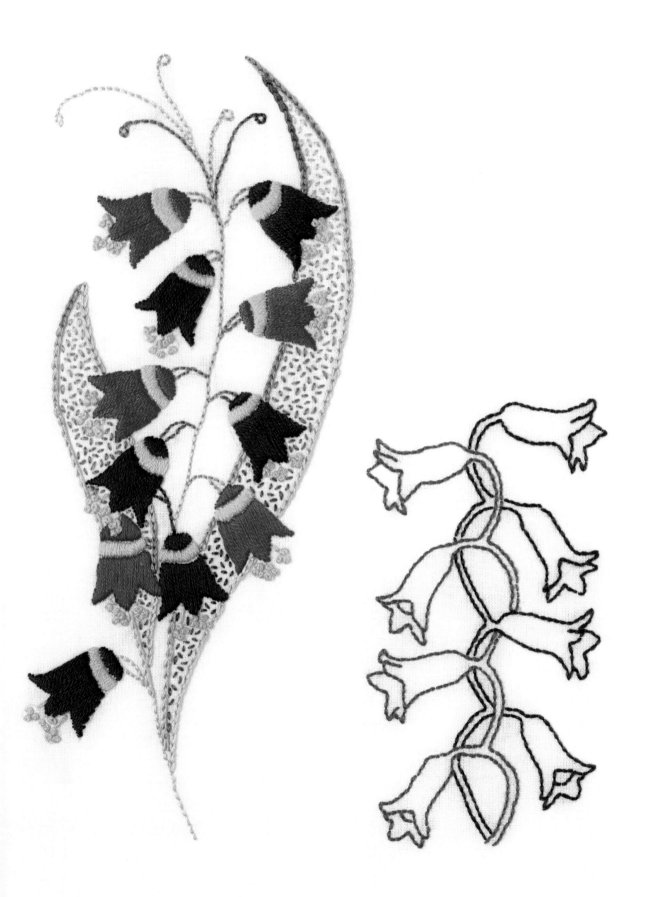

19

Thread key

DMC colours used:

- 726
- 3687
- 3348
- 899
- 48 (var)
- 605
- 818

Stitches and threads used:

Sepals worked with satin stitch using 3 strands of 3348.

Petal folds worked with back stitch using 3 strands of 726.

Petals outlined with chain stitch using 2 strands of 3687.

Stitches and threads used:

Flower centre worked with satin stitch using 899 and 726 (2 strands of each colour).

Petals outlined with back stitch using 2 strands of 48.

Stitches and threads used:

Flower centre worked with satin stitch using 3 strands of 726.

Inner petals and folds on outer petals worked with satin stitch using 3 strands of 605.

Outer petals worked with satin stitch using 3 strands of 818.

20

Thread key

DMC colours used:

- 3777
- 604
- 3687
- 988

Stitches and threads used:

Flower centres worked with French knots and outlined with back stitch using 1 strand of 3777.

Petals outlined with back stitch using either 604 or 3687 (1 strand of each colour).

Leaves worked with satin stitch using 2 strands of 988.

Stems worked with stem stitch using 2 strands of 988.

Stitches and threads used:

Flower centre worked with long stitch (middle) and outlined with back stitch using 1 strand of 3777.

Petals outlined with back stitch using 1 strand of 604.

Stitches and threads used:

Flower centre worked with long stitch (middle) and French knots (left-hand side), and outlined with back stitch, using 1 strand of 3777.

Petals outlined with back stitch using 2 strands of 3687.

21

Thread key

DMC colours used:

■	3799
■	92 (var)
■	4220 (var)
▢	727

Stitches and threads used:

■ Flower centres worked with satin stitch using 3 strands of 3799, and long stitch using 1 strand of 3799.

■ Petals outlined with back stitch using 3 strands of 4220.

■ Leaves worked with satin stitch using 3 strands of 92.

■ Stems worked with stem stitch using 3 strands of 92.

Stitches and threads used:

■ Petals of large flower worked with satin stitch using 3 strands of 4220.

■ Petals of smaller flowers outlined with back stitch using 3 strands of 4220.

▢ Flower centres worked with satin stitch using 3 strands of 727.

■ Circles worked with satin stitch using 3 strands of 92.

Stitches and threads used:

■ Petals outlined with back stitch using 3 strands of 4220.

▢ Flower centre worked with satin stitch using 3 strands of 727.

■ Leaf and stem outlined with back stitch using 3 strands of 92.

22

Stitches and threads used:

■ ■ Petals and leaves outlined with chain stitch using 208 and 704 (2 strands of each colour).

■ Middle petal filled with seed stitch using 2 strands of 704.

■ Flower base, stems and tendrils worked with satin stitch and back stitch using 3 strands of 4025.

Thread key

DMC colours used:

■ 4025 (var)

■ 208

■ 704

■ 4100 (var)

■ 4120 (var)

■ 321

Stitches and threads used:

■ Middle flower outlined with chain stitch and filled with seed stitch using 2 strands of 4100.

■ ■ Outer flowers worked with satin stitch and back stitch using 2 strands of 4120, and decorated with French knots and long stitch using 2 strands of 321.

■ Stems and leaves outlined with back stitch using 2 strands of 704.

Stitches and threads used:

■ Lower flower: petals outlined with chain stitch and decorated with lazy daisy stitch, French knots and back stitch using 2 strands of 4100.

■ ■ Upper flower: as for lower flower, using 2 strands of 4120 for the petals and flower centre, and 2 strands of 321 for the sepals.

■ Stems and veins worked with back stitch; leaves outlined with blanket stitch using 2 strands of 704.

Stitches and threads used:

■ Base and leaves of main flower worked with satin stitch using 3 strands of 4025.

■ Petals of main flower outlined with back stitch using 3 strands of 208.

■ Petals of main flower filled with seed stitch using 3 strands of 704.

■ Stems worked with back stitch using 3 strands of 4025.

23

Stitches and threads used:

 Flowers outlined with back stitch using 3 strands of 4210.

Flowers decorated with seed stitch, satin stitch and French knots using 3 strands of 550.

Leaves worked with satin stitch and stem worked with chain stitch using 3 strands of 4050.

Thread key

DMC colours used:

550

4050 (var)

4210 (var)

4124 (var)

4180 (var)

Stitches and threads used:

Flower outlined with back stitch using 3 strands of 4210.

Flower filled with seed stitch using 3 strands of 550.

Leaves worked with satin stitch using 3 strands of 4050.

Stem worked with back stitch using 3 strands of 4050.

Stitches and threads used:

Flowers and bud worked with satin stitch using 4124 and 4180 using 3 strands of each colour.

Leaves and sepals worked with satin stitch using 3 strands of 4050.

Stems worked with back stitch using 3 strands of 4050.

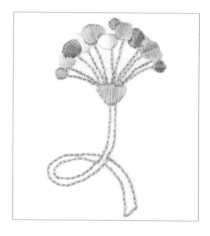

Stitches and threads used:

Flower shapes worked with satin stitch using 4124 and 4180 (3 strands of each colour).

Base of flower worked with satin stitch using 3 strands of 4050.

Stems worked with back stitch using 3 strands of 4050.

24

Thread key

DMC colours used:

■	3052
■	4128 (var)
■	4015 (var)
■	3053
■	4025 (var)
■	4140 (var)

Stitches and threads used:

■ ■ Flowers worked with satin stitch using 4128 and 4025 (3 strands of each colour).

■ Leaves and sepals worked with satin stitch using 3 strands of 3053.

■ Stems worked with back stitch using 3 strands of 4140.

■ Pot worked with satin stitch using 3 strands of 4140.

Stitches and threads used:

■ Buds and flower centres worked with satin stitch using 3 strands of 4128.

■ Flower petals worked with lazy daisy stitch using 3 strands of 4015.

■ Leaves and sepals worked with satin stitch using 3 strands of 3052.

■ Stem worked with back stitch using 3 strands of 3052.

25

Thread key

DMC colours used:

- 726
- 4210 (var)
- 4180 (var)
- 92 (var)

Stitches and threads used:

Four centre petals worked with satin stitch using 3 strands of 4210.

Four small flowers worked with blanket stitch using 3 strands of 4180.

Flower centres worked with satin stitch using 3 strands of 726.

Leaves worked with satin stitch and stems worked with back stitch using 3 strands of 92.

Stitches and threads used:

Flower petals worked with blanket stitch using 4180 and 4210 (3 strands of each colour).

Circles worked with satin stitch using 4180 and 4210 (3 strands of each colour).

Flower centres worked with satin stitch using 3 strands of 726.

Leaves and sepals worked with satin stitch using 3 strands of 92.

Stems worked with back stitch using 3 strands of 92.

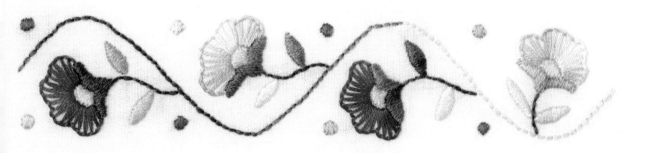

26

Thread key

DMC colours used:

- 4045 (var)
- 743
- 746
- 321

Stitches and threads used:

Flower petals outlined with chain stitch, and petal folds and bud outlined with back stitch using 2 strands of 746.

Flower centre worked with French knots using 3 strands of 743.

Sepals worked with satin stitch using 2 strands of 4045.

Leaves and stems outlined with back stitch using 3 strands of 4045.

Stitches and threads used:

Flower petals outlined with chain stitch, and petal folds worked with back stitch using 2 strands of 746.

Flower centre worked with French knots using 3 strands of 743.

Sepals worked with satin stitch using 2 strands of 4045.

Leaves and stems outlined with back stitch using 3 strands of 4045.

Stitches and threads used:

Flower centre worked with back stitch and a single French knot using 3 strands of 743.

Flower petals worked with back stitch using 2 strands of 746.

Sepals worked with satin stitch using 2 strands of 4045.

Leaves and stem outlined with back stitch using 3 strands of 4045.

Strawberry outlined with chain stitch and filled with lazy daisy stitch using 2 strands of 321.

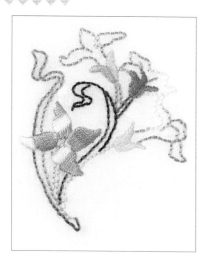 

27

Thread key

DMC colours used:

4150 (var)

92 (var)

4015 (var)

4220 (var)

Stitches and threads used:

Main flower worked with satin stitch, and smaller flowers outlined with back stitch (3 strands of 4220).

Sepals worked with satin stitch (3 strands of 92).

Leaves and stems outlined with back stitch (3 strands of 92).

Stitches and threads used:

Flowers on right worked with satin stitch, and those on left outlined with back stitch (3 strands of 4015).

Leaf and stem worked with satin stitch and back stitch (3 strands of 92).

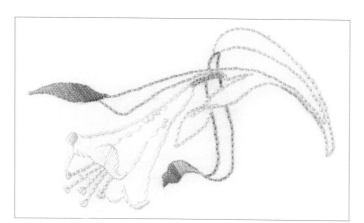

Stitches and threads used:

Flower worked with stem stitch, satin stitch and French knots (3 strands of 4150).

Stamens worked with back stitch (3 strands of 92).

Leaves and stem worked with satin stitch and back stitch (3 strands of 92).

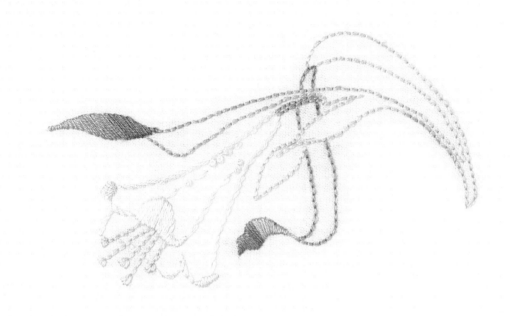

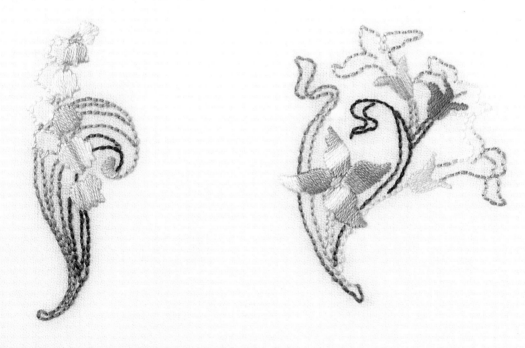

28

Thread key

DMC colours used:

- 115 (var)
- 4200 (var)
- 92 (var)
- 3348
- 4150 (var)
- 4045 (var)

Stitches and threads used:

Flowers worked with satin stitch using 115 and 4200 (3 strands of each colour).

Stems worked with stem stitch (3 strands of 92).

Leaves and veins outlined with back stitch (3 strands of 92).

Base of top flower worked with satin stitch (3 strands of 92).

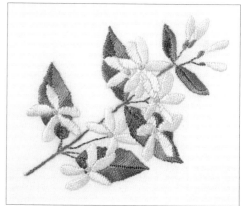

Stitches and threads used:

Flower petals and buds worked with satin stitch (2 strands of 4150).

Flower centres worked with French knots (2 strands of 3348).

Leaves and sepals worked with satin stitch (2 strands of 92).

Stems worked with stem stitch (main stem) and back stitch (smaller stems) (2 strands of 92).

29

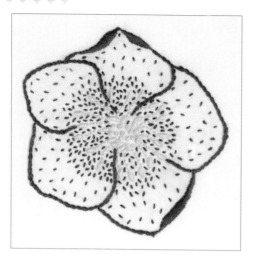

Stitches and threads used:

■ Petals outlined with stem stitch and filled with seed stitch; folds worked with satin stitch (3 strands of 3834).

■ Flower centre worked with French knots (3 strands), surrounded by stamens worked with back stitch and satin stitch (2 strands of 744).

Thread key

DMC colours used:

- ▇ 744
- ▇ 3834
- ▇ 4130 (var)
- ▇ 899
- ▇ 48 (var)
- ▇ 4200 (var)
- ▇ 4050 (var)

Stitches and threads used:

■ Petals outlined with chain stitch (2 strands of 48).

■ Petal folds worked with stem stitch (2 strands of 899).

■ Flower centre worked with French knots (2 strands of 4130).

Stitches and threads used:

■ Petals outlined with back stitch (3 strands of 4200).

■ Flower centre worked with satin stitch (3 strands of 4130).

Stitches and threads used:

■ Petals outlined with back stitch and main folds filled with satin stitch (2 strands of 4050).

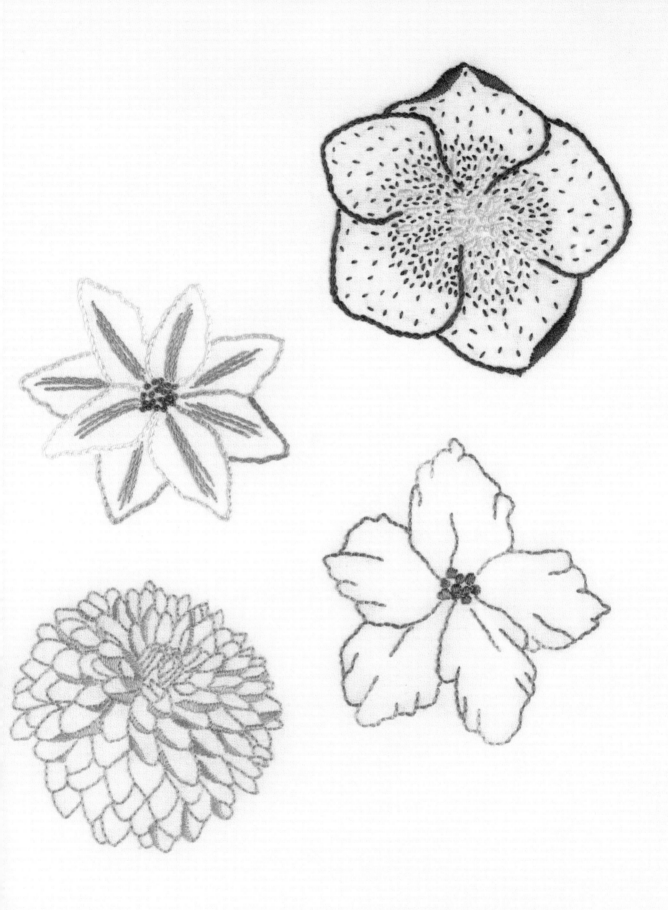

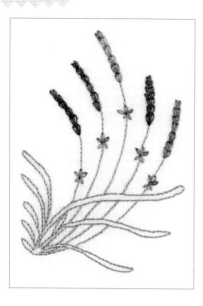

30

Thread key

DMC colours used:

52 (var)

522

Stitches and threads used:

Flowers and sepals worked with lazy daisy stitch using 52 and 522 (1 strand of each colour).

Stems and leaves outlined with back stitch (1 strand of 522).

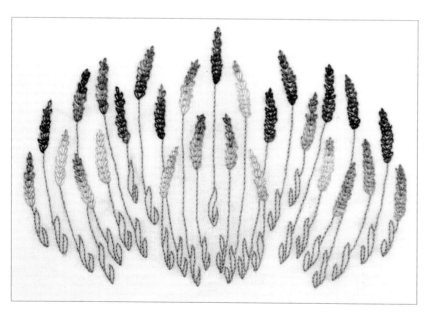

Stitches and threads used:

Flowers worked with lazy daisy stitch (1 strand of 52).

Stems and leaves outlined with back stitch (1 strand of 522).

31

Stitches and threads used:

Flower petals outlined with back stitch using 3 strands of 4128.

Flower centres worked with seed stitch using 3 strands of 4140.

Stem outlined with stem stitch using 2 strands of 4045.

Leaves and veins outlined with back stitch using 3 strands of 4045.

Thread key

DMC colours used:

4128 (var)

4140 (var)

4045 (var)

3857

742

725

368

Stitches and threads used:

Petals worked with satin stitch using 3 strands of 742.

Flower centre worked with French knots using 3 strands of 3857.

Stems and left-hand leaf worked with satin stitch using 3 strands of 4045.

Right-hand leaf outlined with chain stitch (2 strands); fold worked with satin stitch (3 strands); and veins worked with stem stitch (2 strands of 4045).

Stitches and threads used:

Petals worked with satin stitch using 742 (main flower, petal fronts) and 725 (main flower, petal backs and smaller flower) using 2 strands of each colour.

Flower centres worked with French knots and seed stitch using 3 strands of 4140.

Leaves outlined with back stitch using 3 strands of 4045.

Leaf veins outlined with back stitch using 3 strands of 368.

32

DMC colours used:

■	3857
■	4180 (var)
■	899

Stitches and threads used:

■ Stamens worked with satin stitch and stem stitch (2 strands of 3857).

■ Petals outlined with stem stitch (2 strands of 4180).

■ Shading on petals worked with seed stitch (2 strands of 899).

The projects

The following projects show you how you can use the designs to embellish fabric items that you have purchased and want to customise, or may inspire you to make a special gift for a close friend or relative.

As you can see, a huge range of background fabrics can be used, including patterns, stripes, spots, checks and plain. Choose your threads to match the fabric – not just the colours used, but also the thread weight. If you are using a lightweight fabric, choose a relatively fine thread. If the thread is too heavy the fabric may not support the weight of the thread, and if the thread is too thick it will not run through the fabric smoothly.

It is also a good idea to wash your fabric or the item you are going to embroider to allow for shrinkage. The embroidery threads should be colourfast, but you could stitch a small sample to make sure, particularly if you are using a dark-coloured thread on a light background.

Once you have transferred your outline, it needs to be clearly visible on the fabric. If you are using a light-coloured fabric the design can be ironed straight on to it. With darker or heavily patterned fabrics, you could embroider the design on to a piece of plain or lighter-coloured fabric and then sew this to the item. Alternatively, iron the transfer on to water-soluble fabric, then tack it on to the item to be stitched and wash it away when the stitching has been completed (see page 14).

Before you start to stitch, prepare your fabric, either before or after you have transferred the outline, by pressing it lightly with a steam iron to remove any creases. If your fabric has raw edges, you may wish to make a small hem all the way around to help stop them from fraying.

Tea towels

The colours of the designs can be changed to suit the item to be embroidered. The motif used here has been stitched in cream and yellow rather than the oranges and browns used in the sampler.

(See sampler/transfer sheet 29.)

Tea cosy

The border of poppies stitched on to pink gingham has helped to brighten up an otherwise plain tea cosy. Keeping the colour scheme simple has helped to highlight the embroidery. The squares in the gingham have also helped to create a neat row of blanket stitch to finish off the border.

(See sampler/transfer sheet 15.)

Child's sun hat

*The little patch on this sun hat shows
how to use the designs on textured fabric.
The transfer was ironed on to a piece
of cotton fabric and then embroidered
before being appliquéd on to the hat
using blanket stitch.*

(See sampler/transfer sheet 12.)

Greetings cards

Everyone likes to receive a handmade card for a special occasion. If you were making a card for a wedding, you could match the colours to the bridal flowers or the bride's colour scheme. In the case of a birth celebration or baby shower, the colours could be chosen to suit a boy or girl.

(See sampler/transfer sheets 4, 5 and 9.)

The bunting was created by Alistair Macdonald, and appears in his book 20 to Make: Mini Bunting, *published by Search Press, 2013.*

Tote bag

A plain bag can be transformed by adding a decorative panel. When selecting your design, thread colours and background fabric, it is important that these complement the colour of the bag. The cream and black spotty fabric, the black centre of the poppy and the red buttons all help to bring the bag and panel together.

(See sampler/transfer sheet 14.)

Child's denim dress

Adding a little embroidery to this child's pinafore dress has helped to give it a handmade look. The folk style of the design lends itself to the denim very well.

(See sampler/transfer sheet 22.)

Cushion

This bold design has transformed an otherwise plain cushion into an eye-catching accessory for the home.

(See sampler/transfer sheet 16.)

Notebook cover

This pretty cover has transformed an ordinary notebook into something really special that you can give as a gift to friends, family or loved ones – or keep for yourself!

(See sampler/transfer sheet 25.)

Napkins

These napkins would make a lovely addition to an alfresco meal. You could choose to embroider the same design on each one, varying the colours used each time, or to use a different motif on each one.

(See sampler/transfer sheets 22 and 23.)

Lavender bags

Lavender bags are a perennial favourite and make gorgeous little handmade gifts. The heart-shaped motif inspired the smaller lavender bag shown below, and the lavender motif works beautifully on the lavender sleep pillow. The stitching on this little scented pillow uses just one strand of thread to give a very delicate finish.

(See sampler/transfer sheets 1 and 30.)

Needlecase

The colours used on this motif were inspired by a bag of fabric off-cuts, which I used to make this pretty needlecase. Looking at the designs and thread colours alongside your fabric stash can help you choose which to use. For example, you might pick a design that echoes the pattern on the fabric, or thread colours that create a coordinating colour scheme.

(See sampler/transfer sheet 23.)

Pashmina

Choosing the right stitch for the background fabric is important. The seed stitch used on the sampler has been left out of this motif. The weave of the pashmina was too open for the seed stitch to sit properly on the surface.

(See sampler/transfer sheet 32.)

The transfers

Each of the following transfers corresponds to one of the samplers on pages 16–81 and can be used up to ten times. Once they've been removed from the book by cutting carefully round them with scissors, they can be stored in the pocket on the back cover. Make sure you leave as much paper as possible around the outside of the designs.

Note that the ink used on the transfers will fade with washing but may not disappear completely, so, when stitching, follow the printed lines as closely as possible to ensure they are hidden beneath the stitching.

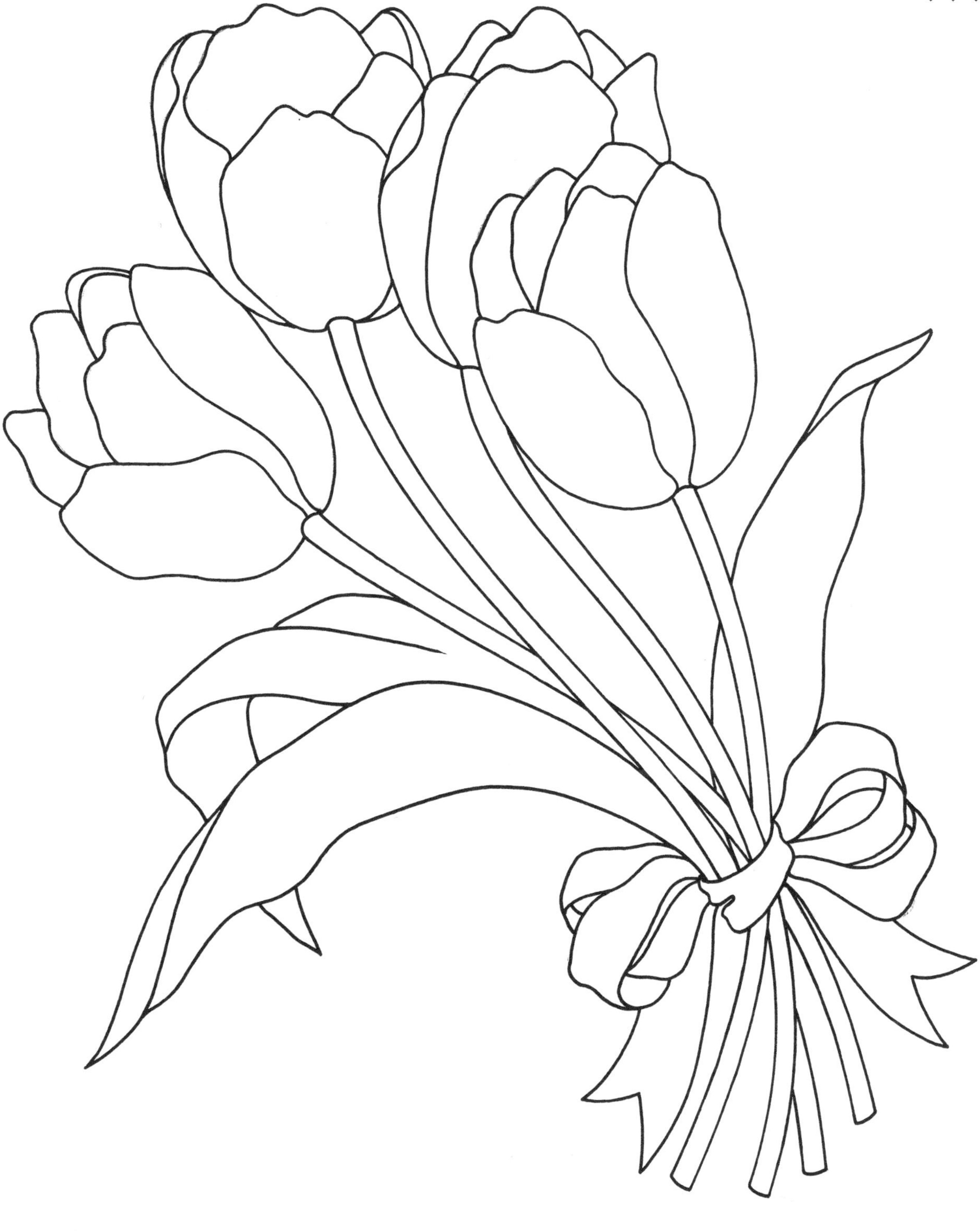

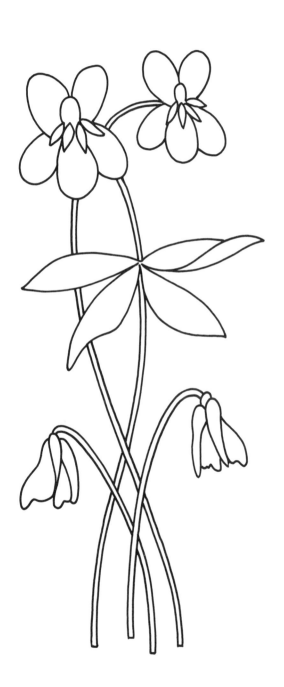

14

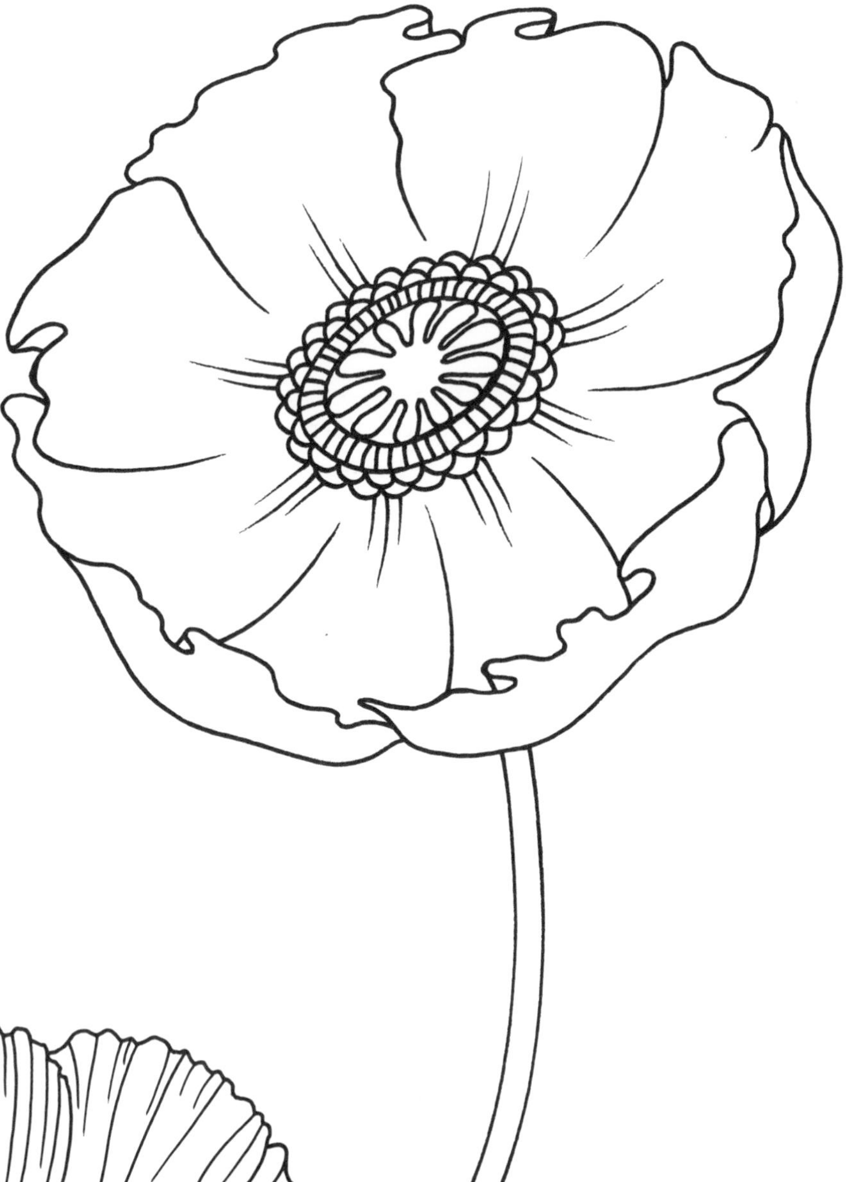

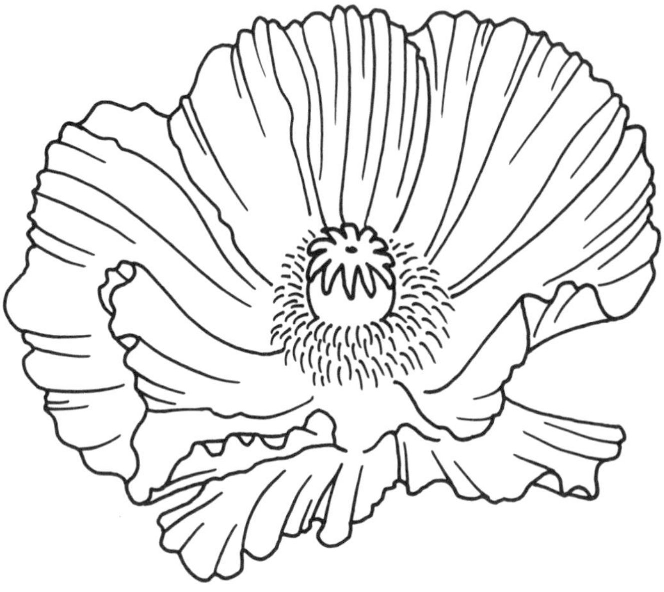

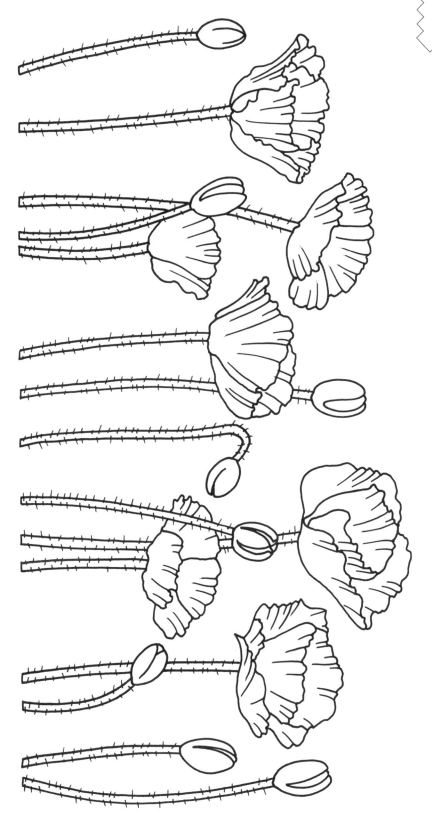

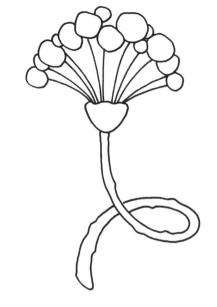

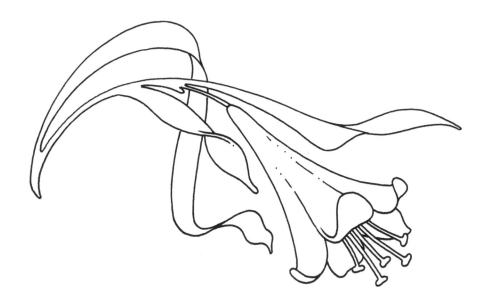

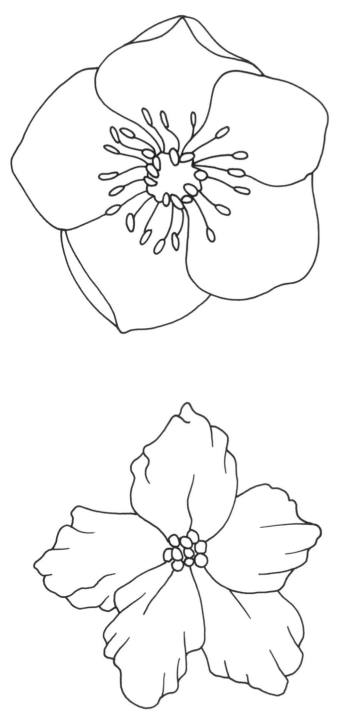

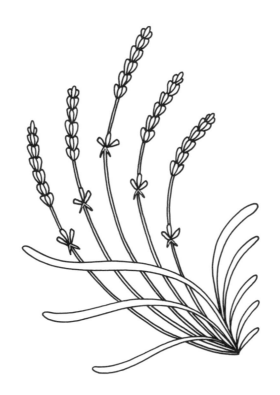

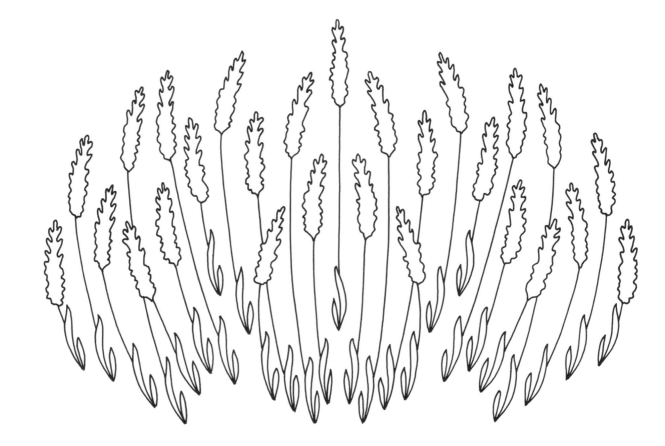

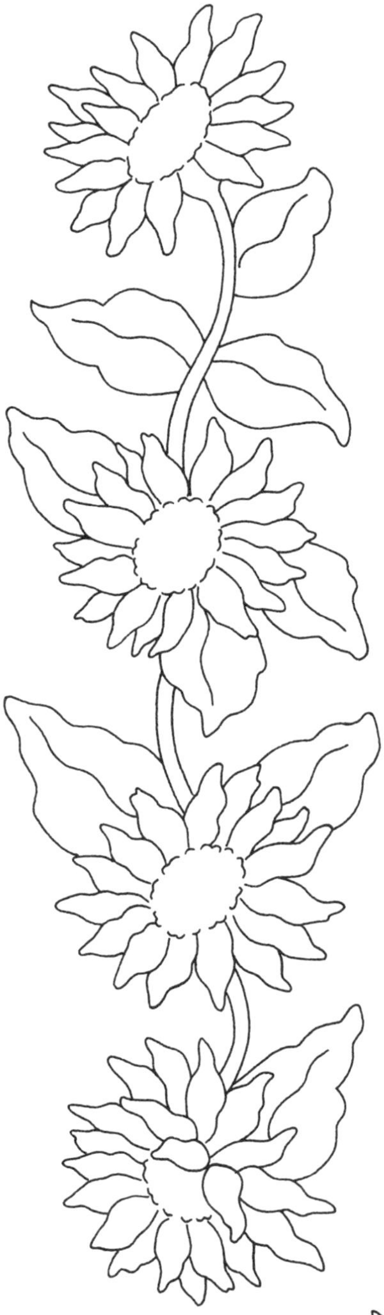

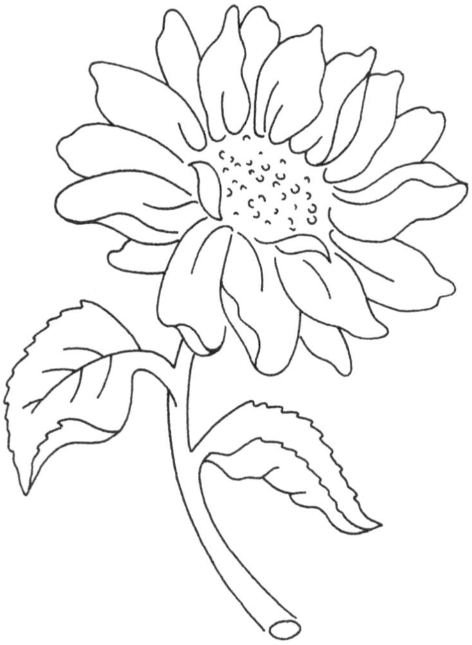